Study Guide for the US Citizenship Test in English and Spanish

Mike Swedenberg

ISBN-13: 978-1983598593
ISBN-10: 1983598593
Translation by Edith DeLeon

Se estudia para convertirse en un ciudadano de los Estados Unidos

Source: U.S. Citizenship and Immigration Services
Fuente: Servicios de la ciudadanía y de la inmigración de Estados Unidos

Contact me at: Mike@Swedenberg.com

Twitter: @USAcitizenship

Study Guide
100 Sample Questions and Answers for the US Immigration Test
in Spanish and English
A unique product, professionally developed and annotated
Updated 2018. / . Actualización 2018

The U.S. Citizenship Services (USCIS) administers a verbal test to all immigrants applying for citizenship. This study guide tutors Spanish speaking immigrants for the USCIS verbal citizenship test in English and Spanish. The questions have been selected from questions used on past exams by the USCIS.

Studying these questions does not guarantee obtaining citizenship to the United States.

Guía de estudio

100 preguntas y respuestas para el nuevo examen de USCIS en inglés y español para el 2011

Un producto único, desarrollado y registrado profesionalmente que será un éxito inmediato en el mercado hispánico.

Los inmigrantes de habla hispana de los profesores particulares para la ciudadanía verbal de USCIS prueban en inglés y español.

Los servicios de la ciudadanía de ESTADOS UNIDOS (USCIS) administran una prueba verbal a todos los inmigrantes que solicitan ciudadanía.

La lista siguiente de 100 preguntas se ha seleccionado de las preguntas usadas encendido más allá de exámenes. Estudiar estas preguntas no garantiza la obtención de ciudadanía
a los Estados Unidos.

TRANSLATOR INTRODUCTION

Hello, my name is Edith DeLeon. I was born in Quito, Ecuador. My parents are Ecuadorians and I'm very proud to be Ecuadorian-American.

I grew up with both cultures. I had the opportunity to study at a college and become a citizen of the United States. I have prospered and I own my home and business in New York and North Carolina. I also work for a company of Certified Public Accountants in the department of information technology for 23 years.

I have a beautiful family, husband and 2 daughters, who also reap the benefits of being born and growing up in the U.S.

One problem with the citizenship test is access to the questions and answers to study. Professor Domiciliary makes this task easier and inexpensive. The professor asked me to help create this new study guide just for you.

Now you have a sample of the questions in Spanish and English.

Thank you very much.
Edith

Hola, mi nombre es Edith DeLeon- nací en Quito, Ecuador. Mis padres son Ecuatorianos.

Yo estoy muy orgullosa de ser Ecuatoriana-Americana, crecí con las dos culturas. Tuve la oportunidad de estudiar en un Colegio y hacerme una ciudadana própera de los E.U.Actualmente vivo y soy propietaria de mi casa y negocios en New York y North Carolina. Tambien trabajo en una Companía de Contadores, en el departamento de tecnologia e información por 23 años.

Tengo una hermosa familia, esposo y 2 hijas, quienes tambien cosechan los beneficios de nacer y crecer en los E.U.

Uno de los problemas es cogar la prueba de la ciudadania,y tener acceso a las preguntas y respuestas para estudiar. El profesor Domiciliario,hace esta tarea mas facil y muy económica. El Profesor me pidió ayuda para crear este nuevo guía de estudio justo para Usted.

Ahora Ud tiene una muestra de las preguntas en Espanól e Ingles.

Muchas Gracias
Edith

ACKNOWLEDGMENTS

We gratefully acknowledge The U.S. Citizenship Services (USCIS) for their cooperation and Mrs. Edith Deleon for her hard work in the translation.

Languages available
Spanish, Polish, French, Portuguese, Russian, Vietnamese, Tagalog, Korean and an English only version.
In Print and eBooks at Amazon.com

CONTENTS

Buy the companion CD where you bought this book.

Study Guide for the US Citizenship Test in English and Spanish CD
Audio CD by Edith DeLeon

"I pledge allegiance to the flag of the United States of America, and to the republic for which it stands, one nation under God, indivisible, with liberty and justice for all."

INTRODUCTION

The 100 sample questions and answers for the US Immigration test are listed below. The test is an oral exam in which the USCIS Officer will ask the applicant up to 10 of the 100 questions. An applicant must answer six out of ten questions correctly to pass the civics portion of the test.

On the naturalization test, some answers may change because of elections or appointments. As you study for the test, make sure that you know the most current members of Congress, Senate, Speaker of the House and Governor of your state and district.

This publication is the only study guide that provides this information and updates it throughout the year.

We also provide you with the Sample Written Questions which all applicants must know how to write in English.

INTRODUCCIÓN

Las 100 preguntas de muestra y sus respuestas para la prueba de Inmigración de EEUU, están listadas abajo. La prueba es un examen oral en el que el Oficial de USCIS le preguntará hasta 10 de las 100 preguntas. Usted debe responder seis de diez preguntas correctamente para pasar la parte de civismo de la prueba. En la prueba de nacionalización, algunas respuestas podrían cambiar debido a las elecciones y nombramientos. A medida que usted estudie para la prueba, asegúrese de que usted conoce la mayoría de miembros actuales del congreso, senado, vocero de la cámara y el gobernador de su estado y distrito.

Esta publicación es la única guía de estudio que provee esta información y la actualiza a lo largo del año. También le proveemos con la muestra de preguntas escritas, que todos los aplicantes deben conocer como escribir en Ingles.

Advice from the Immigration Law offices of Christopher Kurczaba Esq.

6219 N Milwaukee Ave, Chicago, IL 60646

(773) 774-0011

KurczabaLaw@sbcglobal.net

Three Tests for Citizenship

Most applicants for citizenship or naturalization as it is called, are actually subject to THREE different "tests" when applying. It is important that an individual understand that in applying for Citizenship their entire immigration history is being reviewed and an Immigration Officer is making a determination not only over whether an applicant passes a test, but moreover, is reviewing the applicant's entire immigration history.

The Citizenship process should be looked upon as a complex, detailed demanding process, not just the completion of a form and passing of a simple civics test. This is not a process that should be taken lightly. Often persons get "free" help with benevolent charities completing applications during large scale meetings. However, an applicant can face severe consequences including the loss of their permanent residency and even removal from the United States if certain matters come to the attention of an Immigration Officer reviewing your application.

First and foremost are persons who have ever been arrested, detained or even stopped by a Police Officer. These individuals should ensure they seek the assistance of an attorney to review their criminal record before proceeding with the filing of an application for Citizenship.

Each Applicant for Citizenship undergoes three tests:

1. Test of Civics/History/Government, Reading & Writing

a. Civics/history test of 10 questions chosen out of a possible 100

b. Reading – applicants will be asked to read out loud a sample sentence from a fixed set of possible sentences

c. Writing – applicants will be asked to write a sentence dictated by an Immigration Officer.

2. Ability to Communicate in English

a. The Immigration Officer will review your application with you. Traditionally, this takes place after you pass your test. This portion can be difficult for those that do not speak English well.

b. The Immigration Officer will speak to you in English to determine if you generally can communicate.

3. Eligibility –a review of an Applicant's personal history

a. The Immigration Officer will review your entire immigration file and determine if you have the proper character to become a citizen. The Officer will literally have before them your entire immigration history including every form and piece of paper that you submitted to the Immigration Service. This includes your applications for immigration benefits before permanent residency.

i. The Officer will review how you obtained your green card or permanent residency.

1. If you received your permanent residency through marriage to a US Citizen, then the Immigration Officer will ask questions about your marriage. The Officer can question whether the marriage was legitimate.

2. If you received your permanent residency through a family member – the Immigration Officer will review your original application to make sure there were no improprieties when you applied.

3. If you received your permanent residency through an employer – the Immigration Officer can ask you questions about the employer and the employment relationship.

ii. The Officer will review your criminal background – checking if you were ever arrested/detained/stopped by a Police Officer at home or abroad.

1. For the Immigration Service- to be stopped, arrested or detained means precisely that – any time a Police agency would take your fingerprints

a. Regardless of the eventual outcome of the case – or what you think it means to be arrested – you will be expected to admit to all times that you were arrested/stopped or detained by a Police agency.

i. Sometimes applicants believe that an arrest means serving time in jail. But the Immigration Service has a much broader interpretation – including anytime that a Police agency would take your fingerprints and record the information.

ii. The Immigration Service obtains criminal background information on individuals primarily from the FBI. The FBI retains this information forever, regardless of expungements, or local agencies clearing of a criminal history.

Asesoría de las oficinas de inmigración de Christopher Kurczaba
6219 N Milwaukee Ave, Chicago, IL 60646
(773) 774-0011
KurczabaLaw@sbcglobal.net

Tres pruebas para la ciudadanía

La mayoría de los aplicantes a la ciudadanía o nacionalización como se les llama, en realidad son sujetos a TRES pruebas cuando están aplicando. Es importante que un individuo entienda que al aplicar para la Ciudadanía su historial completo de inmigración esta siendo revisado y un Oficial de Inmigración no solo está tomando una decisión sobre si el aplicante pasa una prueba, si no que además esta revisando el historial completo de inmigración del aplicante.

El proceso de Ciudadanía debe ser considerado como un proceso complejo, proceso que demanda detalle, no solo el completado de un formulario y pasar una prueba de civismo. Este es un proceso que no debe tomarse a la ligera. A menudo persona reciben ayuda "gratis" de caridades benevolentes para completar las solicitudes en reuniones a gran escala. Sin embargo, un aplicante puede enfrentar severas consecuencias incluyendo la perdida de su residencia permanente incluso la deportación de los Estados Unidos si ciertas cosas llaman la atención del Oficial de Inmigración que revisa su solicitud. Primero y ante todo personas que alguna vez han sido arrestadas, detenidas o paradas por un Oficial de la Policía. Estos individuos deben asegurarse de buscar asistencia de un abogado para revisar su récord criminal antes de proceder con el llenado de la solicitud de Ciudadanía.

Cada uno de los aplicantes a Ciudadanía se someten a tres pruebas:

1. Prueba de Civismo/Historia/Gobierno, Lectura y Escritura
   a) Prueba de 10 preguntas sobre civismo/historia, elegidas de 100 preguntas posibles.
   b) Lectura: Se le pedirá al solicitante leer en voz alta una oración de muestra de un conjunto de oraciones posibles.
   c) Escritura: Se le pedirá al aplicante que escriba una oración dictada por un Oficial de inmigración.
2. Habilidad para comunicarse en Ingles
   a) El oficial de inmigración revisará su aplicación con usted. Tradicionalmente, esto toma lugar después de que usted pasa su prueba. Esta parte puede ser difícil para aquellos que no hablan bien el ingles.
   b) El Oficial de Inmigración le hablará en Ingles para determinar si usted puede comunicarse generalmente.
3. Elegibilidad: la revisión del historial personal de un aplicante
   a) El Oficial de Inmigración revisará su archivo de inmigración entero y para determinar si usted tiene el carácter adecuado para convertirse en un ciudadano. El Oficial tendrá literalmente enfrente su historial completo de inmigración incluyendo cada formulario y pedazo de papel que usted envió al Servicio de Inmigración. Esto incluye sus solicitudes para beneficios de inmigración antes de la residencia permanente.

i. El oficial revisará como obtuvo su "green card" o su residencia permanente.

1. Si usted recibe su residencia permanente a través de casarse con un ciudadano de Estados Unidos, entonces el Oficial de Inmigración le preguntará sobre su matrimonio. El Oficial puede preguntar si su matrimonio es legítimo.
2. Si usted recibe su residencia permanente a través de un miembro de la familia, el Oficial de Inmigración revisará su solicitud original para asegurarse de que no hubieron inconvenientes cuando aplicó.
3. Si usted recibe su residencia permanente a través de un empleador, el Oficial de Inmigración puede preguntarle sobre el empleador y la relación de empleo.

ii. El Oficial revisará sus antecedentes penales: verificando si usted fue arrestado/detenido/parado por un Oficial de la Policía en el país o en el extranjero.

1. Para el servicio de Inmigración- ser parado, arrestado o detenido significa precisamente eso, cada vez que una agencia de Policía toma sus huellas dactilares.
   a) Independientemente del resultado final del caso,o lo que usted piensa que significa ser arrestado/parado o detenido por una agencia de policía.
      i. A veces los aplicantes piensan que un arresto significa tiempo de servicio en prisión. Pero el Servicio de Inmigración tiene una interpretación más amplia, incluyendo cualquier momento que una agencia de Policía haya tomado sus huellas dactilares y registrado la información.

El Servicio de Inmigración obtiene la información antecedentes penales de los individuos, principalmente del FBI. El FBI retiene esta información para siempre, independientemente sin han sido borrados, o si el historial criminal ha sido limpiado por agencias locales

AMERICAN GOVERNMENT
GOBIERNO AMERICANO

I. Principles of American Democracy / Principios de democracia americana

1. What is the supreme law of the land?

The Constitution

¿Cuál es la legislación nacional suprema?

La constitución

2. What does the Constitution do?

Sets up the government

Defines the government

Protects basic rights of Americans

¿Qué hace la constitución?

Establece el gobierno

Define un gobierno

Protege derechos fundamentales de americanos

3. The idea of self-government is in the first three words of the Constitution. What are these words?

We the People

La idea del gobierno autónomo está en las primeras tres palabras de la constitución. ¿Cuáles son estas palabras?

Nosotros la gente

4. What is an amendment?

A change to the Constitution.

An addition to the Constitution.

¿Cuál es una enmienda?

un cambio a la constitución.

una adición a la constitución.

5. What do we call the first ten amendments to the Constitution?

The Bill of Rights

¿Qué llamamos las primeras diez enmiendas a la constitución?

La Declaración de Derechos

6. What is one right or freedom from the First Amendment? (You need to know one answer)

Speech

Religion

Assembly

Press

Petition the government

¿Cuál es un derecho o libertad de la Primera Enmienda? *(Hay tres respuestas correctas, necesita saber uno)

Discurso

Religion

Asamblea

Prensa

Peticion al gobierno

7. How many amendments does the Constitution have?

Twenty-seven (27)

¿Cuántas enmiendas la constitución tiene?

Veintisiete (27)

8. What did the Declaration of Independence do?

Announced our independence (from Great Britain)

Declared our independence (from Great Britain)

Said that the United States is free (from Great Britain)

¿Qué hizo la Declaración de Independencia?

Anunció nuestra independencia (de Gran Bretaña)

Declaró nuestra independencia (de Gran Bretaña)

Declaro que los Estados Unidos están libres (de Gran Bretaña)

9. What are two rights in the Declaration of Independence?

Life

Liberty

Pursuit of Happiness

¿Cuáles son dos derechos en la Declaración de

Independencia?

Vida

Libertad

Búsqueda de la felicidad

10. What is freedom of religion?

You can practice any religion, or not practice a religion.

¿Cuál es la libertad de religión?

Puedes practicar cualquier religión, o no practicar una religión.

11. What is the economic system in the United States?*

capitalist economy

market economy

¿Cuál es el sistema económico en los Estados Unidos? *

economía capitalista

economía de mercado

12. What is the "rule of law"?

Everyone must follow the law

Leaders must obey the law.

Government must obey the law.

No one is above the law

Cuáles son las " ¿reglas de las leyes "?

Cada uno debe seguir la ley.

Los líderes deben obedecer la ley.

El gobierno debe obedecer la ley.

Nadie está sobre la ley.

System of Government / Sistema de gobierno

13. Name one branch or part of the government.*

Congress

Legislative

President

Executive

The courts

Judicial

Nombre una rama o porción del govierno.*

Congreso

Legislativo

Presidente

Ejecutivo

Las cortes

Judicial

14. What stops one branch of government from becoming too powerful?

Checks and balances

Separation of powers

Qué le detine a una rama de gobierno para llegar hacer demasiado poderoso?

Controles y equilibrios

Separación de poderes

15. Who is in charge of the executive branch?

The President

¿Quién está a cargo del Poder Ejecutivo?

el presidente

16. Who makes federal laws?

Congress

Senate and House (of Representatives)

(U.S. or national) legislature

¿Quién hace las leyes federales?

Congreso

Senado (de representantes)

(los E.E.U.U. o nacional) legislatura

17. What are the two parts of the U.S. Congress?*

The Senate and House (of Representatives)

¿Cuáles son las dos partes del congreso de los E.E.U.U.? *

el Senado y la casa de representantes

18. How many U.S. Senators are there?

One hundred (100)

¿Cuántos senadores de los E.E.U.U. hay?

Cien (100)

19. We elect a U.S. Senator for how many years?

Six (6)

¿Elegimos a senador de los E.E.U.U. por cuántos años?

Seis (6)

20. Who is one of your state's U.S. Senators?*

See List of Representatives in back of book and write the answer here:____

* If you are 65 years old or older and have been a legal permanent resident of the United States for 20 or more years, you may study just the questions that have been marked with an asterisk.

* Si eres 65 años o más y has sido un residente permanente legal de los Estados Unidos por 20 o más años, puedes estudiar apenas las preguntas que se han marcado con un asterisco.

21. The House of Representatives has how many voting members?

Four hundred thirty-five (435)

¿Cuantos miembros votantes tiene La cámara de representantes?

Cuatrocientos treinta y cinco (435)

22. We elect a U.S. Representative for how many years?

Two (2)

¿Elegimos un representante de los E.E.U.U. por cuántos años?

Dos (2)

23. Name your U.S. Representative. (Congressman or Congresswomen)

Answers will vary. [Residents of territories with nonvoting Delegates or resident Commissioners may provide the name of that Delegate or Commissioner. Also acceptable is any statement that the territory has no (voting) Representatives in Congress.]

Nombre tu representante de los E.E.U.U.

Las respuestas variarán. [Los residentes de territorios con los delegados no electorales o los comisionados residentes pueden proporcionar el nombre de ese delegado o comisionado. También aceptable es cualquier declaración que el territorio no tiene ningun(a) representante (de votación) en congreso.]

See List of Representatives in back of book and write the answer here:____

24. Who does a U.S. Senator represent?

All people of the state

¿Quién representa un senador de los E.E.U.U.?

Toda la gente del estado

25. Why do some states have more Representatives than other states?

There are three correct answers. You need to know one answer.

Because of the state's population

Because they have more people

Because some states have more people

¿Por qué algunos estados tienen más representantes que otros estados?

Hay tres respuestas correctas, necesita saber uno.

Debido a la población del estado

Porque tienen más gente

Porque algunos estados tienen más gente

26. We elect a President for how many years?

Four (4)

¿Elegimos a presidente por cuántos años?

Cuatro (4)

27. In what month do we vote for President?*

November

¿En qué mes votamos por un presidente? *

Noviembre

28. What is the name of the President of the United States now?*

President Elect Donald J Trump

¿Cuál es el nombre del Presidente de los Estados Unidos ahora? *

29. What is the name of the Vice President of the United States now?

Vice President Elect Michael R. Pence

¿Cuál es el nombre del vice presidente de los Estados Unidos ahora?

30. If the President can no longer serve, who becomes President?

The Vice President

¿Si el presidente no puede servir más, quien hace de presidente?

El vice presidente

31. If both the President and the Vice President can no longer serve, who becomes President?

The Speaker of the House

¿Si el presidente y el vice presidente no pueden servir más, quien hace de presidente?

El orador de la casa

32. Who is the Commander in Chief of the military?

The President

¿Quién es el comandante y jefe de los militares?

El presidente

33. Who signs bills to become laws?

The President

¿Quién firma propuestas para convertirse en leyes?

El presidente

34. Who vetoes bills?

The President

¿Quién veta propuestas?

El presidente

35. What does the President's Cabinet do?

Advises the President

¿Qué hace el Gabinete del presidente?

Aconseja al presidente

36. What are two Cabinet-level positions?

Secretary of State

Secretary of Labor

Cuáles son dos niveles de posiciones del Cabinete?

El secretario(a) de Estado

El secretario(a) del trabajo

37. What does the judicial branch do?

Reviews laws

Explains laws

Resolves disputes (disagreements)

decides if a law goes against the Constitution

¿Que hace la rama judicial?

Revisar leyes

Explica leyes

Resulven los desacuerdos

Decide si una ley va contra la constitución

38. What is the highest court in the United States?

The Supreme Court

¿Cuál es el tribunal más superior de los Estados Unidos?

El Tribunal Supremo

39. How many justices are on the Supreme Court?

Nine (9)

¿Cuántos jueces hay en el Tribunal Supremo?

Nueve (9)

40. Who is the Chief Justice of the United States?

John G. Roberts, Jr.

¿Quién es el principal jues de los Estados Unidos?

John G. Roberts, Jr.

41. Under our Constitution, some powers belong to the federal government. What is one power of the federal government?

Know one of the following:

To print money

To declare war

To create an army

To make treaties

Bajo nuestra constitución, algunos poderes pertenecen al gobierno federal. ¿Cuál es un poder del gobierno federal?

Conozca una de las siguientes repuestas:

Pra imprimir el dinero

Para declarar guerra

Para crear a un ejército

Para hacer trados

42. Under our Constitution, some powers belong to the states. What is one power of the states?

Provide schooling and education

Bajo nuestra constitución, algunos poderes pertenecen a los estados. ¿Cuál es un poder de los estados?

Proporcionar suficiente educación

43. Who is the Governor of your state?

Answers will vary. Residents of the District of Columbia and U.S. territories without a Governor should say "we don't have a Governor."

¿Quién es el gobernador de tu estado?

Las respuestas variarán. [Los residentes del distrito de Columbia y de los territorios de los E.E.U.U. sin un gobernador deben decir "no tenemos un Gobernador."]

See List of Representatives in back of book and write the answer here:____

44. What is the capital of your state?*

¿Cual es la capital de tu estado? *

Las respuestas variarán. Los residentes del distrito de Columbia deben contestar a que la D.C. no es un estado y no tienen una capital. Los residentes de los territorios de los E.E.U.U. deben nombrar la capital del territorio.

See List of Representatives in back of book and write the answer here:____

45. What are the two major political parties in the United States?*

Democratic and Republican

¿Cuáles son los dos partidos políticos principales en los Estados Unidos? *

Demócratas y Republicanos

46. What is the political party of the President now?

Republican Party

¿Cuál es el partido político del presidente hoy?

Partido Republicano

47. What is the name of the Speaker of the House of Representatives now?

Paul Ryan

¿Cuál es el nombre del Orador de la Cámara de Representantes hoy?

Paul Ryan

C: Rights and Responsibilities

Los derechos y responsabilidades

48. There are four amendments to the Constitution about who can vote. Describe one of them.

Citizens eighteen (18) and older can vote.

Any citizen can vote. (Women and men can vote.)

Hay cuatro enmiendas a la constitución sobre quién puede votar. Describa una de ellas.

Ciudadanos de 18 años o mas puede votar.

Cualquier ciudadano puede votar. (Las mujeres y los hombres pueden votar.)

49. What is one responsibility that is only for United States citizens?*

Serve on a jury

¿Cuál es una responsabilidad que tiene un ciudadano de los Estados Unidos? *

Servir en un jurado

50. What are two rights only for United States citizens?

Apply for a federal job

vote

¿Cuáles son los derechos solamente para los ciudadanos de Estados Unidos?

Solicitar un trabajo federal

Votar

51. What are two rights of everyone living in the United States?

Freedom of expression

Freedom of speech

¿Cuáles son los derechos de cada uno que vive en los Estados Unidos?

Libertad de expresión

Libertad de hablar

52. What do we show loyalty to when we say the Pledge of Allegiance?

The United States and the flag

¿A Qué demostramos lealtad cuando hacemos la jura de la bandera?

A los Estados Unidos y la bandera

53. What is one promise you make when you become a United States citizen?

Defend the Constitution and laws of the United States

¿Cuál es la promesa que haces cuando tú te haces un ciudadano de Estados Unidos?

Defender la constitución y las leyes de los Estados Unidos

54. How old do citizens have to be to vote?*

Eighteen (18) and older

¿ Cual es la edad de un ciudadano para votar? *

Dieciocho (18) años y más

55. What are two ways that Americans can participate in their democracy?

Vote

Join a political party

¿Cuáles son dos maneras que los americanos pueden participar en su democracia?

Votar

Ensamblar un partido político

56. When is the last day you can send in federal income tax forms?*

April 15

¿Cuándo es el ultimo día que tú puedes enviar las formulas de impuesto federal? *

15 de abril

57. When must all men register for the Selective Service?

Between eighteen (18) and twenty-six (26)

¿Cuándo deben registrarse todos los hombres para el servicio selectivo?

Entre dieciocho (18) y veintiséis (26) años

AMERICAN HISTORY / HISTORIA AMERICANA

A: Colonial Period and Independence

Período e independencia coloniales

58. What is one reason colonists came to America?

Freedom

Political liberty

¿ Cuál es una razón que los colonizadores vinieron a América?

Libertad

Libertad política

59. Who lived in America before the Europeans arrived?

Native Americans

American Indians

¿Quién vivió en América antes de que llegaran los europeos?

Nativos americanos

Indios americanos

60. What group of people was taken to America and sold as slaves?

Africans

¿ Qué grupo de personas les vendieron en America como esclavos?

Africanos

61. Why did the colonists fight the British?

Because of high taxes (taxation without representation)

Because the British army stayed in their houses (boarding, quartering)

Because they didn't have self-government

¿Por qué los colonizadores lucharon con los Británicos?

Debido a los altos impuestos (impuestos sin la representación)

Porque el ejército británico permanecía en sus casas (en guardia)

Porque no tenían gobierno autónomo

62. Who wrote the Declaration of Independence?

Thomas Jefferson

¿Quién escribió la Declaración de Independencia?

Thomas Jefferson

63. When was the Declaration of Independence adopted?

July 4, 1776

Cuándo fue adoptada la Declaración de Independencia?

De julio de 1776

64. There were 13 original states. Name three.

New York

New Jersey

Virgina

Había 13 estados originales. Nombre tres.

Nueva York

Nueva Jersey

Virginia

65. What happened at the Constitutional Convention?

The Constitution was written.

¿Qué sucedió en la convención constitucional?

La constitución fue escrita.

66. When was the Constitution written?

1787

¿Cuándo fue escrita la constitución?

1787

67. The Federalist Papers supported the passage of the U.S. Constitution. Name one of the writers.

James Madison

Los papeles federalistas apoyaron el paso de la constitución de los E.E.U.U. Nombre uno de los escritores.

James Madison

68. What is one thing Benjamin Franklin is famous for?

U.S. diplomat

¿Por que fue famoso Benjamin Franklin?

Fue diplomatico de los E.E.U.U.

69. Who is the "Father of Our Country"?

George Washington

Quién es el "¿Padre de nuestro pais"?

George Washington

70. Who was the first President?*

George Washington

¿Quién fue el primer presidente? *

George Washington

71. What territory did the United States buy from France in 1803?

The Louisiana Territory

¿Qué territorio los Estados Unidos compro a Francia en 1803?

El territorio de Luisiana

72. Name one war fought by the United States in the 1800s.

Spanish-American War

Nombre una guerra que los Estados Unidos combatió en los años 1800s.

Guerra hispanoamericana

73. Name the U.S. war between the North and the South.

The Civil War

Nombre la guerra de los E.E.U.U. entre el norte y el sur.

La guerra civil

74. Name one problem that led to the Civil War.

Slavery

Nombre un problema que llevó a la guerra civil.

Esclavitud

75. What was one important thing that Abraham Lincoln did?*

Freed the slaves (Emancipation Proclamation)

¿Que cosa importante hizo Abraham Lincoln? *

Liberó los esclavos (la proclamación de la emancipación)

76. What did the Emancipation Proclamation do?

Freed the slaves

¿Qué hizo la proclamación de la emancipación?

Liberó los esclavos

77. What did Susan B. Anthony do?

Fought for women's rights

¿Qué hizo Susan B. Anthony?

Luchó por los derechos de las mujeres

Recent American History and Other Important Historical Information

La reciente historia americana y otra importante información histórica

78. Name one war fought by the United States in the 1900s.*

World War II

Nombre una guerra de los Estados Unidos en los años 1900s.*

Segunda Guerra Mundial

79. Who was President during World War I?

Woodrow Wilson

¿Quién fue presidente durante la Primera Guerra Mundial?

Woodrow Wilson

80. Who was President during the Great Depression and World War II?

Franklin Roosevelt

¿Quién fue presidente durante la Gran Depresión y la Segunda Guerra Mundial?

Franklin Roosevelt

81. Who did the United States fight in World War II?

Japan, Germany and Italy

¿Con quien peleo los Estados Unidos en la Segunda Guerra Mundial?

Japón, Alemania e Italia

82. Before he was President, Eisenhower was a general. What war was he in?

World War II

Antes que fuera presidente, Eisenhower era un general. ¿En qué guerra estubo él?

Segunda Guerra Mundial

83. During the Cold War, what was the main concern of the United States?

Communism

¿Durante la guerra fría, cuál era la mayor preocupación de los Estados Unidos?

Comunismo

84. What movement tried to end racial discrimination?

civil rights movement

¿Qué movimiento intentó terminar la discriminación racial?

Los derechos civiles (movimiento)

85. What did Martin Luther King, Jr. do?*

Fought for civil rights

¿Qué hizo Martin Luther King, Jr.? *

Luchó por los derechos civiles

86. What major event happened on September 11, 2001 in the United States?

Terrorists attacked the United States.

¿Qué gran evento sucedió el 11 de septiembre de 2001 en los Estados Unidos?

Los terroristas atacaron los Estados Unidos.

87. Name one American Indian tribe in the United States.

Cherokee

Navajo

Apache

Nombre una tribu india americana en los Estados Unidos.

Cherokee

Navajo

Apache

[Adjudicators will be supplied with a complete list.][Suministrarán una lista completa.]

INTEGRATED CIVICS / CíVIC INTEGRADO

Geography /.Geografía

88. Name one of the two longest rivers in the United States.

Missouri or Mississippi river

Nombre uno de los dos ríos más largos en los Estados Unidos.

Rio Missouri o Mississippi

89. What ocean is on the West Coast of the United States?

Pacific Ocean

¿Qué océano está en la costa oeste de los Estados Unidos?

Pacífico

90. What ocean is on the East Coast of the United States?

Atlantic Ocean

¿Qué océano está en la costa este de los Estados Unidos?

Atlántico (océano)

91. Name one U.S. territory.

Puerto Rico

Nombre un territorio de los E.E.U.U..

Puerto Rico

92. Name one state that borders Canada.

New York

Nombre un estado fronterizo con Canadá.

Nueva York

93. Name one state that borders Mexico.

California

Nombre un estado fronterizo con México

California

94. What is the capital of the United States?*

Washington, D.C.

¿Cual ciudad es la capital de los Estados Unidos? *

Washington, D.C.

95. Where is the Statue of Liberty?*

New York Harbor

¿Dónde está la estatua de la libertad? *

En el puerto de Nueva York

Symbols / Símbolos

96. Why does the flag have 13 stripes?

Because there were 13 original colonies

¿Por qué la bandera tiene 13 rayas?

Porque había 13 colonias originales

97. Why does the flag have 50 stars?*

Because there is one star for each state

¿Por qué la bandera tiene 50 estrellas? *

Porque hay una estrella por cada estado

98. What is the name of the national anthem?

The Star-Spangled Banner

¿Cuál es el nombre del himno nacional?

The Star-Spangled Banner

Holidays./.Días de fiesta

99. When do we celebrate Independence Day?*

July 4

¿Cuándo celebramos Día de la Independencia? *

4 de Julio

100. Name two national U.S. holidays.

Independence Day

Christmas

Nombre dos días de fiesta nacionales de los E.E.U.U.

Día de la independencia

La Navidad

Sample Written Sentences

You will be asked to write a sample sentence. Normally you can make up to three (3) errors in writing and still pass the test.
Be careful to listen to each word the examiner reads. Make sure to write each word, even if you think it is not needed grammatically, if the examiner reads a word; please write out every word that is dictated.

1) A senator is elected for 6 years.

2) Michael Pence is the Vice President of the United States.

3) All people want to be free.

4) America is the land of freedom.

5) All American citizens have the right to vote.

6) America is the home of the brave.

7) America is the land of the free.

8) Donald J Trump is the President of the United States.

9) Citizens have the right to vote.

10) Congress is part of the American government.

11) Congress meets in Washington DC.

12) Congress passes laws in the United States.

13) George Washington was the first president.

14) I want to be a citizen of the United States.

15) I want to be an American citizen.

16) I want to become an American so I can vote.

17) It is important for all citizens to vote.

18) Many people come to America for freedom.

19) Many people have died for freedom.

20) Martha Washington was the first lady.

21) Only Congress can declare war.

22) Our Government is divided into three branches.

23) People in America have the right to freedom.

24) People vote for the President in November.

25) The American flag has stars and stripes.

26) The American flag has 13 stripes.

27) The capital of the United States is Washington DC.

28) The colors of the flag are red white and blue.

29) The Constitution is the supreme law of our land.

30) The flag of the United States has 50 stars.

31) The House and Senate are parts of Congress

32) The President enforces the laws.

33) The President has the power of veto.

34) The President is elected every 4 years.

35) The President lives in the White House.

36) The President lives in Washington D.C.

37) The President must be an American citizen.

38) The President must be born in the United States.

39) The President signs bills into law.

40) The stars of the American flag are white.

41) The White House is in Washington, DC.

42) The United States flag is red white and blue.

43) The United States of America has 50 states.

List of Representatives and Capitals

Members of the Senate

Representatives are subject to change.

Find your state to identify your two Senators

Source: http://Senate.gov Updated January 2018

What is a class? - Article I, section 3 of the Constitution requires the Senate to be divided into three classes for purposes of elections. Senators are elected to six-year terms, and every two years the members of one class—approximately one-third of the senators—face election or reelection. Terms for senators in Class I expire in 2019, Class II in 2021, and Class III in 2023.

U.S. State Postal Abbreviations List

Alabama – AL Alaska – AK Arizona – AZ Arkansas - AR

California – CA Colorado – CO Connecticut - CT

Delaware – DE District of Columbia - DC

Florida - FL

Georgia - GA

Hawaii - HI

Idaho – ID Illinois – IL Indiana – IN Iowa - IA

Kansas – KS Kentucky - KY

Louisiana - LA

Maine – ME Maryland – MD Massachusetts – MA Michigan – MI Minnesota – MN Mississippi – MS Missouri – MO Montana - MT

Nebraska – NE   Nevada – NV   New Hampshire – NH   New Jersey – NJ   New Mexico – NM   New York – NY   North Carolina – NC   North Dakota - ND

Ohio – OH   Oklahoma – OK   Oregon - OR

Pennsylvania - PA

Rhode Island - RI

South Carolina – SC   South Dakota - SD

Tennessee – TN   Texas - TX

Utah - UT

Vermont – VT   Virginia - VA

Washington – WA   West Virginia – WV   Wisconsin – WI   Wyoming - WY

US Commonwealth and Territories

American Samoa – AS   Federated States of Micronesia – FM   Guam – GU   Marshall Islands - MH

Northern Mariana Islands – MP   Palau – PW   Puerto Rico – PR   Virgin Islands

Senators of the 115th Congress

Murkowski, Lisa - (R - AK) Class III

522 Hart Senate Office Building Washington DC 20510

(202) 224-6665

Contact: www.murkowski.senate.gov/public/index.cfm/contact

Sullivan, Dan - (R - AK) Class II

702 Hart Senate Office Building Washington DC 20510

(202) 224-3004

Contact: www.sullivan.senate.gov/contact/email

Shelby, Richard C. - (R - AL) Class III

304 Russell Senate Office Building Washington DC 20510

(202) 224-5744

Contact: www.shelby.senate.gov/public/index.cfm/emailsenatorshelby

Strange, Luther - (R - AL) Class II **(To be replaced by Doug Jones)**

326 Russell Senate Office Building Washington DC 20510

(202) 224-4124

Contact: www.strange.senate.gov/content/contact-senator

Boozman, John - (R - AR) Class III

141 Hart Senate Office Building Washington DC 20510

(202) 224-4843

Contact: www.boozman.senate.gov/public/index.cfm/contact

Cotton, Tom - (R - AR) Class II

124 Russell Senate Office Building Washington DC 20510

(202) 224-2353

Contact: www.cotton.senate.gov/?p=contact

Flake, Jeff - (R - AZ) Class I

413 Russell Senate Office Building Washington DC 20510

(202) 224-4521

Contact: www.flake.senate.gov/public/index.cfm/contact-jeff

McCain, John - (R - AZ) Class III

218 Russell Senate Office Building Washington DC 20510

(202) 224-2235

Contact: www.mccain.senate.gov/public/index.cfm/contact-form

Feinstein, Dianne - (D - CA) Class I

331 Hart Senate Office Building Washington DC 20510

(202) 224-3841

Contact: www.feinstein.senate.gov/public/index.cfm/e-mail-me

Harris, Kamala D. - (D - CA) Class III

112 Hart Senate Office Building Washington DC 20510

(202) 224-3553

Contact: www.harris.senate.gov/contact

Bennet, Michael F. - (D - CO) Class III

261 Russell Senate Office Building Washington DC 20510

(202) 224-5852

Contact: www.bennet.senate.gov/?p=contact

Gardner, Cory - (R - CO) Class II

354 Russell Senate Office Building Washington DC 20510

(202) 224-5941

Contact: www.gardner.senate.gov/contact-cory/email-cory

Blumenthal, Richard - (D - CT) Class III

706 Hart Senate Office Building Washington DC 20510

(202) 224-2823

Contact: www.blumenthal.senate.gov/contact/

Murphy, Christopher - (D - CT) Class I

136 Hart Senate Office Building Washington DC 20510

(202) 224-4041

Contact: www.murphy.senate.gov/contact

Carper, Thomas R. - (D - DE) Class I

513 Hart Senate Office Building Washington DC 20510

(202) 224-2441

Contact: www.carper.senate.gov/public/index.cfm/email-senator-carper

Coons, Christopher A. - (D - DE) Class II

127A Russell Senate Office Building Washington DC 20510

(202) 224-5042

Contact: www.coons.senate.gov/contact

Nelson, Bill - (D - FL) Class I

716 Hart Senate Office Building Washington DC 20510

(202) 224-5274

Contact: www.billnelson.senate.gov/contact-bill

Rubio, Marco - (R - FL) Class III

284 Russell Senate Office Building Washington DC 20510

(202) 224-3041

Contact: www.rubio.senate.gov/public/index.cfm/contact

Isakson, Johnny - (R - GA) Class III

131 Russell Senate Office Building Washington DC 20510

(202) 224-3643

Contact: www.isakson.senate.gov/public/index.cfm/email-me

Perdue, David - (R - GA) Class II

455 Russell Senate Office Building Washington DC 20510

(202) 224-3521

Contact: www.perdue.senate.gov/connect/email

Hirono, Mazie K. - (D - HI) Class I

730 Hart Senate Office Building Washington DC 20510

(202) 224-6361

Contact: www.hirono.senate.gov/contact

Schatz, Brian - (D - HI) Class III

722 Hart Senate Office Building Washington DC 20510

(202) 224-3934

Contact: www.schatz.senate.gov/contact

Ernst, Joni - (R - IA) Class II

111 Russell Senate Office Building Washington DC 20510

(202) 224-3254

Contact: www.ernst.senate.gov/public/index.cfm/contact

Grassley, Chuck - (R - IA) Class III

135 Hart Senate Office Building Washington DC 20510

(202) 224-3744

Contact: www.grassley.senate.gov/contact

Crapo, Mike - (R - ID) Class III

239 Dirksen Senate Office Building Washington DC 20510

(202) 224-6142

Contact: www.crapo.senate.gov/contact

Risch, James E. - (R - ID) Class II

483 Russell Senate Office Building Washington DC 20510

(202) 224-2752

Contact: www.risch.senate.gov/public/index.cfm?p=Email

Duckworth, Tammy - (D - IL) Class III

524 Hart Senate Office Building Washington DC 20510

(202) 224-2854

Contact: www.duckworth.senate.gov/content/contact-senator

Durbin, Richard J. - (D - IL) Class II

711 Hart Senate Office Building Washington DC 20510

(202) 224-2152

Contact: www.durbin.senate.gov/contact/

Donnelly, Joe - (D - IN) Class I

720 Hart Senate Office Building Washington DC 20510

(202) 224-4814

Contact: www.donnelly.senate.gov/contact/email-joe

Young, Todd - (R - IN) Class III

400 Russell Senate Office Building Washington DC 20510

(202) 224-5623

Contact: www.young.senate.gov/contact

Moran, Jerry - (R - KS) Class III

521 Dirksen Senate Office Building Washington DC 20510

(202) 224-6521

Contact: www.moran.senate.gov/public/index.cfm/e-mail-jerry

Roberts, Pat - (R - KS) Class II

109 Hart Senate Office Building Washington DC 20510

(202) 224-4774

Contact: www.roberts.senate.gov/public/?p=EmailPat

McConnell, Mitch - (R - KY) Class II

317 Russell Senate Office Building Washington DC 20510

(202) 224-2541

Contact: www.mcconnell.senate.gov/public/index.cfm?p=contact

Paul, Rand - (R - KY) Class III

167 Russell Senate Office Building Washington DC 20510

(202) 224-4343

Contact: www.paul.senate.gov/connect/email-rand

Cassidy, Bill - (R - LA) Class II

520 Hart Senate Office Building Washington DC 20510

(202) 224-5824

Contact: www.cassidy.senate.gov/contact

Kennedy, John - (R - LA) Class III

383 Russell Senate Office Building Washington DC 20510

(202) 224-4623

Contact: www.kennedy.senate.gov/public/email-me

Markey, Edward J. - (D - MA) Class II

255 Dirksen Senate Office Building Washington DC 20510

(202) 224-2742

Contact: www.markey.senate.gov/contact

Warren, Elizabeth - (D - MA) Class I

317 Hart Senate Office Building Washington DC 20510

(202) 224-4543

Contact: www.warren.senate.gov/?p=email_senator

Cardin, Benjamin L. - (D - MD) Class I

509 Hart Senate Office Building Washington DC 20510

(202) 224-4524

Contact: www.cardin.senate.gov/contact/

Van Hollen, Chris - (D - MD) Class III

110 Hart Senate Office Building Washington DC 20510

(202) 224-4654

Contact: www.vanhollen.senate.gov/content/contact-senator

Collins, Susan M. - (R - ME) Class II

413 Dirksen Senate Office Building Washington DC 20510

(202) 224-2523

Contact: www.collins.senate.gov/contact

King, Angus S., Jr. - (I - ME) Class I

133 Hart Senate Office Building Washington DC 20510

(202) 224-5344

Contact: www.king.senate.gov/contact

Peters, Gary C. - (D - MI) Class II

724 Hart Senate Office Building Washington DC 20510

(202) 224-6221

Contact: www.peters.senate.gov/contact/email-gary

Stabenow, Debbie - (D - MI) Class I

731 Hart Senate Office Building Washington DC 20510

(202) 224-4822

Contact: www.stabenow.senate.gov/contact

Franken, Al - (D - MN) Class II **(Tentative resignation to be replaced by a yet named person)**

309 Hart Senate Office Building Washington DC 20510

(202) 224-5641

Contact: www.franken.senate.gov/?p=contact

Klobuchar, Amy - (D - MN) Class I

302 Hart Senate Office Building Washington DC 20510

(202) 224-3244

Contact: www.klobuchar.senate.gov/public/index.cfm/contact

Blunt, Roy - (R - MO) Class III

260 Russell Senate Office Building Washington DC 20510

(202) 224-5721

Contact: www.blunt.senate.gov/public/index.cfm/contact-roy

McCaskill, Claire - (D - MO) Class I

503 Hart Senate Office Building Washington DC 20510

(202) 224-6154

Contact: www.mccaskill.senate.gov/contact

Cochran, Thad - (R - MS) Class II

113 Dirksen Senate Office Building Washington DC 20510

(202) 224-5054

Contact: www.cochran.senate.gov/public/index.cfm/email-me

Wicker, Roger F. - (R - MS) Class I

555 Dirksen Senate Office Building Washington DC 20510

(202) 224-6253

Contact: www.wicker.senate.gov/public/index.cfm/contact

Daines, Steve - (R - MT) Class II

320 Hart Senate Office Building Washington DC 20510

(202) 224-2651

Contact: www.daines.senate.gov/connect/email-steve

Tester, Jon - (D - MT) Class I

311 Hart Senate Office Building Washington DC 20510

(202) 224-2644

Contact: www.tester.senate.gov/?p=email_senator

Burr, Richard - (R - NC) Class III

217 Russell Senate Office Building Washington DC 20510

(202) 224-3154

Contact: www.burr.senate.gov/contact/email

Tillis, Thom - (R - NC) Class II

185 Dirksen Senate Office Building Washington DC 20510

(202) 224-6342

Contact: www.tillis.senate.gov/public/index.cfm/email-me

Heitkamp, Heidi - (D - ND) Class I

516 Hart Senate Office Building Washington DC 20510

(202) 224-2043

Contact: www.heitkamp.senate.gov/public/index.cfm/contact

Hoeven, John - (R - ND) Class III

338 Russell Senate Office Building Washington DC 20510

(202) 224-2551

Contact: www.hoeven.senate.gov/public/index.cfm/email-the-senator

Fischer, Deb - (R - NE) Class I

454 Russell Senate Office Building Washington DC 20510

(202) 224-6551

Contact: www.fischer.senate.gov/public/index.cfm/contact

Sasse, Ben - (R - NE) Class II

136 Russell Senate Office Building Washington DC 20510

(202) 224-4224

Contact: www.sasse.senate.gov/public/index.cfm/email-ben

Hassan, Margaret Wood - (D - NH) Class III

330 Hart Senate Office Building Washington DC 20510

(202) 224-3324

Contact: www.hassan.senate.gov/content/contact-senator

Shaheen, Jeanne - (D - NH) Class II

506 Hart Senate Office Building Washington DC 20510

(202) 224-2841

Contact: www.shaheen.senate.gov/contact/contact-jeanne

Booker, Cory A. - (D - NJ) Class II

359 Dirksen Senate Office Building Washington DC 20510

(202) 224-3224

Contact: www.booker.senate.gov/?p=contact

Menendez, Robert - (D - NJ) Class I

528 Hart Senate Office Building Washington DC 20510

(202) 224-4744

Contact: www.menendez.senate.gov/contact

Heinrich, Martin - (D - NM) Class I

303 Hart Senate Office Building Washington DC 20510

(202) 224-5521

Contact: www.heinrich.senate.gov/contact

Udall, Tom - (D - NM) Class II

531 Hart Senate Office Building Washington DC 20510

(202) 224-6621

Contact: www.tomudall.senate.gov/?p=contact

Cortez Masto, Catherine - (D - NV) Class III

204 Russell Senate Office Building Washington DC 20510

(202) 224-3542

Contact: www.cortezmasto.senate.gov/contact

Heller, Dean - (R - NV) Class I

324 Hart Senate Office Building Washington DC 20510

(202) 224-6244

Contact: www.heller.senate.gov/public/index.cfm/contact-form

Gillibrand, Kirsten E. - (D - NY) Class I

478 Russell Senate Office Building Washington DC 20510

(202) 224-4451

Contact: www.gillibrand.senate.gov/contact/email-me

Schumer, Charles E. - (D - NY) Class III

322 Hart Senate Office Building Washington DC 20510

(202) 224-6542

Contact: www.schumer.senate.gov/contact/email-chuck

Brown, Sherrod - (D - OH) Class I

713 Hart Senate Office Building Washington DC 20510

(202) 224-2315

Contact: www.brown.senate.gov/contact/

Portman, Rob - (R - OH) Class III

448 Russell Senate Office Building Washington DC 20510

(202) 224-3353

Contact: www.portman.senate.gov/public/index.cfm/contact?p=contact...

Inhofe, James M. - (R - OK) Class II

205 Russell Senate Office Building Washington DC 20510

(202) 224-4721

Contact: www.inhofe.senate.gov/contact

Lankford, James - (R - OK) Class III

316 Hart Senate Office Building Washington DC 20510

(202) 224-5754

Contact: www.lankford.senate.gov/contact/email

Merkley, Jeff - (D - OR) Class II

313 Hart Senate Office Building Washington DC 20510

(202) 224-3753

Contact: www.merkley.senate.gov/contact/

Wyden, Ron - (D - OR) Class III

221 Dirksen Senate Office Building Washington DC 20510

(202) 224-5244

Contact: www.wyden.senate.gov/contact/

Casey, Robert P., Jr. - (D - PA) Class I

393 Russell Senate Office Building Washington DC 20510

(202) 224-6324

Contact: www.casey.senate.gov/contact/

Toomey, Patrick J. - (R - PA) Class III

248 Russell Senate Office Building Washington DC 20510

(202) 224-4254

Contact: www.toomey.senate.gov/?p=contact

Reed, Jack - (D - RI) Class II

728 Hart Senate Office Building Washington DC 20510

(202) 224-4642

Contact: www.reed.senate.gov/contact/

Whitehouse, Sheldon - (D - RI) Class I

530 Hart Senate Office Building Washington DC 20510

(202) 224-2921

Contact: www.whitehouse.senate.gov/contact/email-sheldon

Graham, Lindsey - (R - SC) Class II

290 Russell Senate Office Building Washington DC 20510

(202) 224-5972

Contact: www.lgraham.senate.gov/public/index.cfm/e-mail-senator-gr...

Scott, Tim - (R - SC) Class III

717 Hart Senate Office Building Washington DC 20510

(202) 224-6121

Contact: www.scott.senate.gov/contact/email-me

Rounds, Mike - (R - SD) Class II

502 Hart Senate Office Building Washington DC 20510

(202) 224-5842

Contact: www.rounds.senate.gov/contact/email-mike

Thune, John - (R - SD) Class III

511 Dirksen Senate Office Building Washington DC 20510

(202) 224-2321

Contact: www.thune.senate.gov/public/index.cfm/contact

Alexander, Lamar - (R - TN) Class II

455 Dirksen Senate Office Building Washington DC 20510

(202) 224-4944

Contact: www.alexander.senate.gov/public/index.cfm?p=Email

Corker, Bob - (R - TN) Class I

425 Dirksen Senate Office Building Washington DC 20510

(202) 224-3344

Contact: www.corker.senate.gov/public/index.cfm/emailme

Cornyn, John - (R - TX) Class II

517 Hart Senate Office Building Washington DC 20510

(202) 224-2934

Contact: www.cornyn.senate.gov/contact

Cruz, Ted - (R - TX) Class I

404 Russell Senate Office Building Washington DC 20510

(202) 224-5922

Contact: www.cruz.senate.gov/?p=form&id=16

Hatch, Orrin G. - (R - UT) Class I

104 Hart Senate Office Building Washington DC 20510

(202) 224-5251

Contact: www.hatch.senate.gov/public/index.cfm/contact?p=Email-Orrin

Lee, Mike - (R - UT) Class III

361A Russell Senate Office Building Washington DC 20510

(202) 224-5444

Contact: www.lee.senate.gov/public/index.cfm/contact

Kaine, Tim - (D - VA) Class I

231 Russell Senate Office Building Washington DC 20510

(202) 224-4024

Contact: www.kaine.senate.gov/contact

Warner, Mark R. - (D - VA) Class II

703 Hart Senate Office Building Washington DC 20510

(202) 224-2023

Contact: www.warner.senate.gov/public/index.cfm?p=Contact

Leahy, Patrick J. - (D - VT) Class III

437 Russell Senate Office Building Washington DC 20510

(202) 224-4242

Contact: www.leahy.senate.gov/contact/

Sanders, Bernard - (I - VT) Class I

332 Dirksen Senate Office Building Washington DC 20510

(202) 224-5141

Contact: www.sanders.senate.gov/contact/

Cantwell, Maria - (D - WA) Class I

511 Hart Senate Office Building Washington DC 20510

(202) 224-3441

Contact: www.cantwell.senate.gov/public/index.cfm/email-maria

Murray, Patty - (D - WA) Class III

154 Russell Senate Office Building Washington DC 20510

(202) 224-2621

Contact: www.murray.senate.gov/public/index.cfm/contactme

Baldwin, Tammy - (D - WI) Class I

709 Hart Senate Office Building Washington DC 20510

(202) 224-5653

Contact: www.baldwin.senate.gov/feedback

Johnson, Ron - (R - WI) Class III

328 Hart Senate Office Building Washington DC 20510

(202) 224-5323

Contact: www.ronjohnson.senate.gov/public/index.cfm/email-the-sena...

Capito, Shelley Moore - (R - WV) Class II

172 Russell Senate Office Building Washington DC 20510

(202) 224-6472

Contact: www.capito.senate.gov/contact/contact-shelley

Manchin, Joe, III - (D - WV) Class I

306 Hart Senate Office Building Washington DC 20510

(202) 224-3954

Contact: www.manchin.senate.gov/public/index.cfm/contact-form

Barrasso, John - (R - WY) Class I

307 Dirksen Senate Office Building Washington DC 20510

(202) 224-6441

Contact: www.barrasso.senate.gov/public/index.cfm/contact-form

Enzi, Michael B. - (R - WY) Class II

379A Russell Senate Office Building Washington DC 20510

(202) 224-3424

Contact: http://www.enzi.senate.gov/public/index.cfm/contact?p=e-mail-senator-enzi

Find your state and your District Number to identify your Representative

Members of the 115th Congress

Find your state and your District Number to identify your Congressperson. You must determine what district you live in to identify your Representative.

Updated January 2018

Source: http://www.house.gov/representatives/

Alabama

District	Name	Party	Room	Phone
1	Byrne, Bradley	R	119 CHOB	202-225-4931
2	Roby, Martha	R	442 CHOB	202-225-2901
3	Rogers, Mike	R	2184 RHOB	202-225-3261
4	Aderholt, Robert	R	235 CHOB	202-225-4876
5	Brooks, Mo	R	2400 RHOB	202-225-4801
6	Palmer, Gary	R	330 CHOB	202-225-4921
7	Sewell, Terri A.	D	2201 RHOB	202-225-2665

Alaska

District	Name	Party	Room	Phone
At Large	Young, Don	R	2314 RHOB	202-225-5765

American Samoa

District	Name	Party	Room	Phone
At Large	Radewagen, Amata	R	1339 LHOB	202-225-8577

Arizona

District	Name	Party	Room	Phone
1	O'Halleran, Tom	D	126 CHOB	202-225-3361
2	McSally, Martha	R	510 CHOB	202-225-2542

3 Grijalva, Raul D 1511 LHOB 202-225-2435
4 Gosar, Paul A. R 2057 RHOB 202-225-2315
5 Biggs, Andy R 1626 LHOB 202-225-2635
6 Schweikert, David R 2059 RHOB 202-225-2190
7 Gallego, Ruben D 1218 LHOB 202-225-4065
8 Franks, TrentR 2435 RHOB 202-225-4576
9 Sinema, Kyrsten D 1725 LHOB 202-225-9888

Arkansas

District Name Party Room Phone
1 Crawford, Rick R 2422 RHOB 202-225-4076
2 Hill, French R 1229 LHOB 202-225-2506
3 Womack, Steve R 2412 RHOB 202-225-4301
4 Westerman, Bruce R 130 CHOB 202-225-3772

California

District Name Party Room Phone
1 LaMalfa, Doug R 322 CHOB 202-225-3076
2 Huffman, Jared D 1406 LHOB 202-225-5161
3 Garamendi, John D 2438 RHOB 202-225-1880
4 McClintock, TomR 2312 RHOB 202-225-2511
5 Thompson, Mike D 231 CHOB 202-225-3311
6 Matsui, Doris O. D 2311 RHOB 202-225-7163
7 Bera, Ami D 1431 LHOB 202-225-5716
8 Cook, Paul R 1222 LHOB 202-225-5861
9 McNerney, Jerry D 2265 RHOB 202-225-1947
10 Denham, Jeff R 1730 LHOB 202-225-4540
11 DeSaulnier, MarkD 115 CHOB 202-225-2095
12 Pelosi, Nancy D 233 CHOB 202-225-4965
13 Lee, Barbara D 2267 RHOB 202-225-2661
14 Speier, Jackie D 2465 RHOB 202-225-3531
15 Swalwell, Eric D 129 CHOB 202-225-5065
16 Costa, Jim D 2081 RHOB 202-225-3341
17 Khanna, Ro D 513 CHOB 202-225-2631
18 Eshoo, Anna G. D 241 CHOB 202-225-8104
19 Lofgren, Zoe D 1401 LHOB 202-225-3072
20 Panetta, Jimmy D 228 CHOB 202-225-2861

21 Valadao, David R 1728 LHOB 202-225-4695
22 Nunes, Devin R 1013 LHOB 202-225-2523
23 McCarthy, Kevin R 2421 RHOB 202-225-2915
24 Carbajal, Salud D 212 CHOB 202-225-3601
25 Knight, Steve R 1023 LHOB 202-225-1956
26 Brownley, Julia D 1019 LHOB 202-225-5811
27 Chu, Judy D 2423 RHOB 202-225-5464
28 Schiff, AdamD 2372 RHOB 202-225-4176
29 Cárdenas, Tony D 1510 LHOB 202-225-6131
30 Sherman, Brad D 2181 RHOB 202-225-5911
31 Aguilar, Pete D 1223 LHOB 202-225-3201
32 Napolitano, Grace D 1610 LHOB 202-225-5256
33 Lieu, Ted D 236 CHOB 202-225-3976
34 Gomez, Jimmy D 1226 LHOB (202) 225-6235
35 Torres, Norma D 1713 LHOB 202-225-6161
36 Ruiz, Raul D 1319 LHOB 202-225-5330
37 Bass, Karen D 2241 RHOB 202-225-7084
38 Sánchez, Linda D 2329 RHOB 202-225-6676
39 Royce, Ed R 2310 RHOB 202-225-4111
40 Roybal-Allard, Lucille D 2083 RHOB 202-225-1766
41 Takano, Mark D 1507 LHOB 202-225-2305
42 Calvert, Ken R 2205 RHOB 202-225-1986
43 Waters, Maxine D 2221 RHOB 202-225-2201
44 Barragán, Nanette D 1320 LHOB 202-225-8220
45 Walters, Mimi R 215 CHOB 202-225-5611
46 Correa, J. Luis D 1039 LHOB 202-225-2965
47 Lowenthal, Alan D 125 CHOB 202-225-7924
48 Rohrabacher, Dana R 2300 RHOB 202-225-2415
49 Issa, Darrell R 2269 RHOB 202-225-3906
50 Hunter, Duncan D. R 2429 RHOB 202-225-5672
51 Vargas, Juan D 1605 LHOB 202-225-8045
52 Peters, Scott D 1122 LHOB 202-225-0508
53 Davis, Susan D 1214 LHOB 202-225-2040

Colorado

District Name Party Room Phone
1 DeGette, Diana D 2111 RHOB 202-225-4431
2 Polis, Jared D 1727 LHOB 202-225-2161

3 Tipton, Scott R 218 CHOB 202-225-4761
4 Buck, Ken R 1130 LHOB 202-225-4676
5 Lamborn, Doug R 2402 RHOB 202-225-4422
6 Coffman, Mike R 2443 RHOB 202-225-7882
7 Perlmutter, Ed D 1410 LHOB 202-225-2645

Connecticut

District Name Party Room Phone
1 Larson, John B. D 1501 LHOB 202-225-2265
2 Courtney, Joe D 2348 RHOB 202-225-2076
3 DeLauro, Rosa L.D 2413 RHOB 202-225-3661
4 Himes, Jim D 1227 LHOB 202-225-5541
5 Esty, Elizabeth D 221 CHOB 202-225-4476

Delaware

District Name Party Room Phone
At Large Blunt Rochester, Lisa D 1123 LHOB
202-225-4165

District of Columbia

District Name Party Room Phone
At Large Norton, Eleanor HolmesD 2136 RHOB 202-225-8050

Florida

District Name Party Room Phone
1 Gaetz, Matt R 507 CHOB 202-225-4136
2 Dunn, Neal R 423 CHOB 202-225-5235
3 Yoho, Ted R 511 CHOB 202-225-5744
4 Rutherford, John R 230 CHOB 202-225-2501
5 Lawson, Al D 1337 LHOB 202-225-0123
6 DeSantis, Ron R 1524 LHOB 202-225-2706
7 Murphy, Stephanie D 1237 LHOB 202-225-4035
8 Posey, Bill R 2150 RHOB 202-225-3671
9 Soto, Darren D 1429 LHOB 202-225-9889
10 Demings, Val D 238 CHOB 202-225-2176

11 Webster, Daniel R 1210 LHOB 202-225-1002
12 Bilirakis, Gus M. R 2112 RHOB 202-225-5755
13 Crist, CharlieD 427 CHOB 202-225-5961
14 Castor, Kathy D 2052 RHOB 202-225-3376
15 Ross, Dennis R 436 CHOB 202-225-1252
16 Buchanan, Vern R 2104 RHOB 202-225-5015
17 Rooney, Tom R 2160 RHOB 202-225-5792
18 Mast, Brian R 2182 RHOB 202-225-3026
19 Rooney, Francis R 120 CHOB 202-225-2536
20 Hastings, Alcee L. D 2353 RHOB 202-225-1313
21 Frankel, Lois D 1037 LHOB 202-225-9890
22 Deutch, Ted D 2447 RHOB 202-225-3001
23 Wasserman Schultz, Debbie D 1114 LHOB 202-225-7931
24 Wilson, FredericaD 2445 RHOB 202-225-4506
25 Diaz-Balart, Mario R 440 CHOB 202-225-4211
26 Curbelo, Carlos R 1404 LHOB 202-225-2778
27 Ros-Lehtinen, Ileana R 2206 RHOB 202-225-3931

Georgia

District Name Party Room Phone
1 Carter, Buddy R 432 CHOB 202-225-5831
2 Bishop Jr., Sanford D. D 2407 RHOB 202-225-3631
3 Ferguson, A. Drew R 1032 LHOB 202-225-5901
4 Johnson, Henry C. "Hank" Jr. D 2240 RHOB 202-225-1605
5 Lewis, John D 343 CHOB 202-225-3801
6 Price, Tom R 1211 LHOB 202-225-4501
7 Woodall, Robert R 1724 LHOB 202-225-4272
8 Scott, Austin R 2417 RHOB 202-225-6531
9 Collins, Doug R 1504 LHOB 202-225-9893
10 Hice, Jody R 324 CHOB 202-225-4101
11 Loudermilk, Barry R 329 CHOB 202-225-2931
12 Allen, Rick R 426 CHOB 202-225-2823
13 Scott, David D 225 CHOB 202-225-2939
14 Graves, Tom R 2078 RHOB 202-225-5211

Guam

District	Name	Party	Room	Phone
At Large	Bordallo, Madeleine	D	2441 RHOB	202-225-1188

Hawaii

District	Name	Party	Room	Phone
1	Hanabusa, Colleen	D	422 CHOB	202-225-2726
2	Gabbard, Tulsi	D	1433 LHOB	202-225-4906

Idaho

District	Name	Party	Room	Phone
1	Labrador, Raul R.	R	1523 LHOB	202-225-6611
2	Simpson, Mike	R	2084 RHOB	202-225-5531

Illinois

District	Name	Party	Room	Phone
1	Rush, Bobby L.	D	2188 RHOB	202-225-4372
2	Kelly, Robin	D	1239 LHOB	202-225-0773
3	Lipinski, Daniel	D	2346 RHOB	202-225-5701
4	Gutierrez, Luis	D	2408 RHOB	202-225-8203
5	Quigley, Mike	D	2458 RHOB	202-225-4061
6	Roskam, Peter J.	R	2246 RHOB	202-225-4561
7	Davis, Danny K.	D	2159 RHOB	202-225-5006
8	Krishnamoorthi, Raja	D	515 CHOB	202-225-3711
9	Schakowsky, Jan	D	2367 RHOB	202-225-2111
10	Schneider, Bradley	D	1432 LHOB	202-225-4835
11	Foster, Bill	D	1224 LHOB	202-225-3515
12	Bost, Mike	R	1440 LHOB	202-225-5661
13	Davis, Rodney	R	1740 LHOB	202-225-2371
14	Hultgren, Randy	R	2455 RHOB	202-225-2976
15	Shimkus, John	R	2217 RHOB	202-225-5271
16	Kinzinger, Adam	R	2245 RHOB	202-225-3635

17	Bustos, Cheri	D	1009 LHOB	202-225-5905
18	LaHood,Darin	R	1424 LHOB	202-225-6201

Indiana

District	Name	Party	Room	Phone
1	Visclosky, Peter	D	2328 RHOB	202-225-2461
2	Walorski, Jackie	R	419 CHOB	202-225-3915
3	Banks, Jim	R	509 CHOB	202-225-4436
4	Rokita, Todd	R	2439 RHOB	202-225-5037
5	Brooks, Susan W.	R	1030 LHOB	202-225-2276
6	Messer, Luke	R	1230 LHOB	202-225-3021
7	Carson, André	D	2135 RHOB	202-225-4011
8	Bucshon, Larry	R	1005 LHOB	202-225-4636
9	Hollingsworth, Trey	R	1641 LHOB	202-225-5315

Iowa

District	Name	Party	Room	Phone
1	Blum, Rod	R	1108 LHOB	202-225-2911
2	Loebsack, David	D	1527 LHOB	202-225-6576
3	Young, David	R	240 CHOB	202-225-5476
4	King, Steve	R	2210 RHOB	202-225-4426

Kansas

District	Name	Party	Room	Phone
1	Marshall, Roger	R	312 CHOB	202-225-2715
2	Jenkins, Lynn	R	1526 LHOB	202-225-6601
3	Yoder, Kevin	R	2433 RHOB	202-225-2865
4	Estes, Ron	R	2452 RHOB	(202) 225-6216

Kentucky

District	Name	Party	Room	Phone
1	Comer, James	R	1513 LHOB	202-225-3115
2	Guthrie, S. Brett	R	2434 RHOB	202-225-3501
3	Yarmuth, John A.	D	131 CHOB	202-225-5401
4	Massie, Thomas	R	2453 RHOB	202-225-3465

5 Rogers, Harold R 2406 RHOB 202-225-4601
6 Barr, Andy R 1427 LHOB 202-225-4706

Louisiana

District	Name	Party	Room	Phone
1	Scalise, Steve	R	2338 RHOB	202-225-3015
2	Richmond, Cedric	D	420 CHOB	202-225-6636
3	Higgins, Clay	R	1711 LHOB	202-225-2031
4	Johnson, Mike	R	327 CHOB	202-225-2777
5	Abraham, Ralph	R	417 CHOB	202-225-8490
6	Graves, Garret	R	430 CHOB	202-225-3901

Maine

District	Name	Party	Room	Phone
1	Pingree, Chellie	D	2162 RHOB	202-225-6116
2	Poliquin, Bruce	R	1208 LHOB	202-225-6306

Maryland

District	Name	Party	Room	Phone
1	Harris, Andy	R	1533 LHOB	202-225-5311
2	Ruppersberger, C. A. Dutch	D	2416 RHOB	202-225-3061
3	Sarbanes, John P.	D	2444 RHOB	202-225-4016
4	Brown, Anthony	D	1505 LHOB	202-225-8699
5	Hoyer, Steny H.	D	1705 LHOB	202-225-4131
6	Delaney, John	D	1632 LHOB	202-225-2721
7	Cummings, Elijah	D	2163 RHOB	202-225-4741
8	Raskin, Jamie	D	431 CHOB	202-225-5341

Massachusetts

District	Name	Party	Room	Phone
1	Neal, Richard E.	D	341 CHOB	202-225-5601
2	McGovern, James	D	438 CHOB	202-225-6101
3	Tsongas, Niki	D	1714 LHOB	202-225-3411
4	Kennedy III, Joseph P.	D	434 CHOB	202-225-5931
5	Clark, Katherine	D	1415 LHOB	202-225-2836

6	Moulton, Seth	D	1408 LHOB	202-225-8020
7	Capuano, Michael E.	D	1414 LHOB	202-225-5111
8	Lynch, Stephen F.	D	2268 RHOB	202-225-8273
9	Keating, William	D	2351 RHOB	202-225-3111

Michigan

District	Name	Party	Room	Phone
1	Bergman, Jack	R	414 CHOB	202-225-4735
2	Huizenga, Bill	R	2232 RHOB	202-225-4401
3	Amash, Justin	R	114 CHOB	202-225-3831
4	Moolenaar, John	R	117 CHOB	202-225-3561
5	Kildee, Daniel	D	227 CHOB	202-225-3611
6	Upton, Fred	R	2183 RHOB	202-225-3761
7	Walberg, Tim	R	2436 RHOB	202-225-6276
8	Bishop, Mike	R	428 CHOB	202-225-4872
9	Levin, Sander	D	1236 LHOB	202-225-4961
10	Mitchell, Paul	R	211 CHOB	202-225-2106
11	Trott, Dave	R	1722 LHOB	202-225-8171
12	Dingell, Debbie	D	116 CHOB	202-225-4071
13	Conyers Jr., John	D	2426 RHOB	202-225-5126
14	Lawrence, Brenda	D	1213 LHOB	202-225-5802

Minnesota

District	Name	Party	Room	Phone
1	Walz, Timothy J.	D	2313 RHOB	202-225-2472
2	Lewis, Jason	R	418 CHOB	202-225-2271
3	Paulsen, Erik	R	127 CHOB	202-225-2871
4	McCollum, Betty	D	2256 RHOB	202-225-6631
5	Ellison, Keith	D	2263 RHOB	202-225-4755
6	Emmer, Tom	R	315 CHOB	202-225-2331
7	Peterson, Collin C.	D	2204 RHOB	202-225-2165
8	Nolan, Rick	D	2366 RHOB	202-225-6211

Mississippi

District	Name	Party	Room	Phone
1	Kelly, Trent	R	1721 LHOB	202-225-4306

District	Name	Party	Room	Phone
2	Thompson, Bennie G.	D	2466 RHOB	202-225-5876
3	Harper, Gregg	R	2227 RHOB	202-225-5031
4	Palazzo, Steven	R	2349 RHOB	202-225-5772

Missouri

District	Name	Party	Room	Phone
1	Clay Jr., William "Lacy"	D	2428 RHOB	202-225-2406
2	Wagner, Ann	R	435 CHOB	202-225-1621
3	Luetkemeyer, Blaine	R	2230 RHOB	202-225-2956
4	Hartzler, Vicky	R	2235 RHOB	202-225-2876
5	Cleaver, Emanuel	D	2335 RHOB	202-225-4535
6	Graves, Sam	R	1135 LHOB	202-225-7041
7	Long, Billy	R	2454 RHOB	202-225-6536
8	Smith, Jason	R	1118 LHOB	202-225-4404

Montana

District	Name	Party	Room	Phone
At Large	Gianforte, Greg	R	1419 LHOB	(202) 225-3211

Nebraska

District	Name	Party	Room	Phone
1	Fortenberry, Jeff	R	1514 LHOB	202-225-4806
2	Bacon, Don	R	1516 LHOB	202-225-4155
3	Smith, Adrian	R	320 CHOB	202-225-6435

Nevada

District	Name	Party	Room	Phone
1	Titus, Dina	D	2464 RHOB	202-225-5965
2	Amodei, Mark	R	332 CHOB	202-225-6155
3	Rosen, Jacky	D	413 CHOB	202-225-3252
4	Kihuen, Ruben	D	313 CHOB	202-225-9894

New Hampshire

District	Name	Party	Room	Phone
1	Shea-Porter, Carol	D	1530 LHOB	202-225-5456
2	Kuster, Ann	D	137 CHOB	202-225-5206

New Jersey

District	Name	Party	Room	Phone
1	Norcross, Donald	D	1531 LHOB	202-225-6501
2	LoBiondo, Frank	R	2427 RHOB	202-225-6572
3	MacArthur, Tom	R	506 CHOB	202-225-4765
4	Smith, Chris	R	2373 RHOB	202-225-3765
5	Gottheimer, Josh	D	213 CHOB	202-225-4465
6	Pallone Jr., Frank	D	237 CHOB	202-225-4671
7	Lance, Leonard	R	2352 RHOB	202-225-5361
8	Sires, Albio	D	2342 RHOB	202-225-7919
9	Pascrell Jr., Bill	D	2370 RHOB	202-225-5751
10	Payne Jr., Donald	D	132 CHOB	202-225-3436
11	Frelinghuysen, Rodney	R	2306 RHOB	202-225-5034
12	Watson Coleman, Bonnie	D	1535 LHOB	202-225-5801

New Mexico

District	Name	Party	Room	Phone
1	Lujan Grisham, Michelle	D	214 CHOB	202-225-6316
2	Pearce, Steve	R	2432 RHOB	202-225-2365
3	Lujan, Ben R.	D	2231 RHOB	202-225-6190

New York

District	Name	Party	Room	Phone
1	Zeldin, Lee	R	1517 LHOB	202-225-3826
2	King, Pete	R	339 CHOB	202-225-7896
3	Suozzi, Thomas	D	226 CHOB	202-225-3335
4	Rice, Kathleen	D	1508 LHOB	202-225-5516
5	Meeks, Gregory W.	D	2234 RHOB	202-225-3461
6	Meng, Grace	D	1317 LHOB	202-225-2601

7 Velázquez, Nydia M. D 2302 RHOB 202-225-2361
8 Jeffries, Hakeem D 1607 LHOB 202-225-5936
9 Clarke, Yvette D. D 2058 RHOB 202-225-6231
10 Nadler, Jerrold D 2109 RHOB 202-225-5635
11 Donovan, Daniel R 1541 LHOB 202-225-3371
12 Maloney, Carolyn D 2308 RHOB 202-225-7944
13 Espaillat, Adriano D 1630 LHOB 202-225-4365
14 Crowley, Joseph D 1035 LHOB 202-225-3965
15 Serrano, José E. D 2354 RHOB 202-225-4361
16 Engel, Eliot D 2462 RHOB 202-225-2464
17 Lowey, Nita D 2365 RHOB 202-225-6506
18 Maloney, Sean Patrick D 1027 LHOB 202-225-5441
19 Faso, John R 1616 LHOB 202-225-5614
20 Tonko, Paul D. D 2463 RHOB 202-225-5076
21 Stefanik, Elise R 318 CHOB 202-225-4611
22 Tenney, Claudia R 512 CHOB 202-225-3665
23 Reed, Tom R 2437 RHOB 202-225-3161
24 Katko, John R 1620 LHOB 202-225-3701
25 Slaughter, Louise D 2469 RHOB 202-225-3615
26 Higgins, Brian D 2459 RHOB 202-225-3306
27 Collins, Chris R 1117 LHOB 202-225-5265

North Carolina

District Name Party Room Phone
1 Butterfield, G.K. D 2080 RHOB 202-225-3101
2 Holding, George R 1110 LHOB 202-225-3032
3 Jones, Walter B. R 2333 RHOB 202-225-3415
4 Price, David D 2108 RHOB 202-225-1784
5 Foxx, Virginia R 2262 RHOB 202-225-2071
6 Walker, Mark R 1305 LHOB 202-225-3065
7 Rouzer, David R 424 CHOB 202-225-2731
8 Hudson, Richard R 429 CHOB 202-225-3715
9 Pittenger, Robert R 224 CHOB 202-225-1976
10 McHenry, Patrick T. R 2334 RHOB 202-225-2576
11 Meadows, Mark R 1024 LHOB 202-225-6401
12 Adams, Alma D 222 CHOB 202-225-1510
13 Budd, Ted R 118 CHOB 202-225-4531

North Dakota

District	Name	Party	Room	Phone
At Large	Cramer, Kevin	R	1717 LHOB	202-225-2611

Northern Mariana Islands

District	Name	Party	Room	Phone
At Large	Sablan, Gregorio	D	2411 RHOB	202-225-2646

Ohio

District	Name	Party	Room	Phone
1	Chabot, Steve	R	2371 RHOB	202-225-2216
2	Wenstrup, Brad	R	2419 LHOB	202-225-3164
3	Beatty, Joyce	D	133 CHOB	202-225-4324
4	Jordan, Jim	R	2056 RHOB	202-225-2676
5	Latta, Robert E.	R	2448 RHOB	202-225-6405
6	Johnson, Bill	R	1710 LHOB	202-225-5705
7	Gibbs, Bob	R	2446 RHOB	202-225-6265
8	Davidson, Warren	R	1004 LHOB	202-225-6205
9	Kaptur, Marcy	D	2186 RHOB	202-225-4146
10	Turner, Michael	R	2368 RHOB	202-225-6465
11	Fudge, Marcia L.	D	2344 RHOB	202-225-7032
12	Tiberi, Pat	R	1203 LHOB	202-225-5355
13	Ryan, Tim	D	1126 LHOB	202-225-5261
14	Joyce, David	R	1124 LHOB	202-225-5731
15	Stivers, Steve	R	1022 LHOB	202-225-2015
16	Renacci, Jim	R	328 CHOB	202-225-3876

Oklahoma

District	Name	Party	Room	Phone
1	Bridenstine, Jim	R	216 CHOB	202-225-2211
2	Mullin, Markwayne	R	1113 LHOB	202-225-2701
3	Lucas, Frank	R	2405 RHOB	202-225-5565
4	Cole, Tom	R	2467 RHOB	202-225-6165
5	Russell, Steve	R	128 CHOB	202-225-2132

Oregon

District Name Party Room Phone
1 Bonamici, Suzanne D 439 CHOB 202-225-0855
2 Walden, Greg R 2185 RHOB 202-225-6730
3 Blumenauer, Earl D 1111 LHOB 202-225-4811
4 DeFazio, Peter D 2134 RHOB 202-225-6416
5 Schrader, Kurt D 2431 RHOB 202-225-5711

Pennsylvania

District Name Party Room Phone
1 Brady, Robert D 2004 RHOB 202-225-4731
2 Evans, Dwight D 1105 LHOB 202-225-4001
3 Kelly, Mike R 1707 LHOB 202-225-5406
4 Perry, Scott R 1207 LHOB 202-225-5836
5 Thompson, Glenn W. R 124 CHOB 202-225-5121
6 Costello, Ryan R 326 CHOB 202-225-4315
7 Meehan, Pat R 2305 RHOB 202-225-2011
8 Fitzpatrick, Brian R 514 CHOB 202-225-4276
9 Shuster, Bill R 2079 RHOB 202-225-2431
10 Marino, Tom R 2242 RHOB 202-225-3731
11 Barletta, Lou R 2049 RHOB 202-225-6511
12 Rothfus, Keith R 1205 LHOB 202-225-2065
13 Boyle, Brendan D 1133 LHOB 202-225-6111
14 Doyle, Mike D 239 CHOB 202-225-2135
15 Dent, Charles W. R 2082 RHOB 202-225-6411
16 Smucker, Lloyd R 516 CHOB 202-225-2411
17 Cartwright, Matthew D 1034 LHOB 202-225-5546
18 Murphy, Tim R 2332 RHOB 202-225-2301
Puerto Rico

District Name Party Room Phone
At Large González-Colón, Jenniffer R 1529 LHOB 202-225-2615

Rhode Island

District Name Party Room Phone

1 Cicilline, David D 2244 RHOB 202-225-4911
2 Langevin, Jim D 2077 RHOB 202-225-2735

South Carolina

District Name Party Room Phone
1 Sanford, Mark R 2211 RHOB 202-225-3176
2 Wilson, Joe R 1436 LHOB 202-225-2452
3 Duncan, Jeff R 2229 RHOB 202-225-5301
4 Gowdy, Trey R 2418 RHOB 202-225-6030
5 Norman, Ralph R 2350 RHOB (202) 225-5501
6 Clyburn, James E. D 242 CHOB 202-225-3315
7 Rice, Tom R 223 CHOB 202-225-9895

South Dakota

District Name Party Room Phone
At LargeNoem, Kristi R 2457 RHOB 202-225-2801
Tennessee

District Name Party Room Phone
1 Roe, Phil R 336 CHOB 202-225-6356
2 Duncan Jr., John J. R 2207 RHOB 202-225-5435
3 Fleischmann, Chuck R 2410 RHOB 202-225-3271
4 DesJarlais, Scott R 2301 RHOB 202-225-6831
5 Cooper, Jim D 1536 LHOB 202-225-4311
6 Black, Diane R 1131 LHOB 202-225-4231
7 Blackburn, Marsha R 2266 RHOB 202-225-2811
8 Kustoff, David R 508 CHOB 202-225-4714
9 Cohen, Steve D 2404 RHOB 202-225-3265

Texas

District Name Party Room Phone
1 Gohmert, Louie R 2243 RHOB 202-225-3035
2 Poe, TedR 2132 RHOB 202-225-6565
3 Johnson, Sam R 2304 RHOB 202-225-4201
4 Ratcliffe, John R 325 CHOB 202-225-6673
5 Hensarling, Jeb R 2228 RHOB 202-225-3484

6 Barton, Joe R 2107 RHOB 202-225-2002
7 Culberson, John R 2161 RHOB 202-225-2571
8 Brady, KevinR 1011 LHOB 202-225-4901
9 Green, Al D 2347 RHOB 202-225-7508
10 McCaul, Michael T. R 2001 RHOB 202-225-2401
11 Conaway, K. Michael R 2430 RHOB 202-225-3605
12 Granger, Kay R 1026 LHOB 202-225-5071
13 Thornberry, Mac R 2208 RHOB 202-225-3706
14 Weber, Randy R 1708 LHOB 202-225-2831
15 Gonzalez, Vicente D 113 CHOB 202-225-2531
16 O'Rourke, Beto D 1330 LHOB 202-225-4831
17 Flores, Bill R 2440 RHOB 202-225-6105
18 Jackson Lee, Sheila D 2187 RHOB 202-225-3816
19 Arrington, Jodey R 1029 LHOB 202-225-4005
20 Castro, Joaquin D 1221 LHOB 202-225-3236
21 Smith, Lamar R 2409 RHOB 202-225-4236
22 Olson, Pete R 2133 RHOB 202-225-5951
23 Hurd, Will R 317 CHOB 202-225-4511
24 Marchant, Kenny R 2369 RHOB 202-225-6605
25 Williams, Roger R 1323 LHOB 202-225-9896
26 Burgess, Michael R 2336 RHOB 202-225-7772
27 Farenthold, BlakeR 2331 RHOB 202-225-7742
28 Cuellar, Henry D 2209 RHOB 202-225-1640
29 Green, Gene D 2470 RHOB 202-225-1688
30 Johnson, Eddie Bernice D 2468 RHOB 202-225-8885
31 Carter, John R 2110 RHOB 202-225-3864
32 Sessions, Pete R 2233 RHOB 202-225-2231
33 Veasey, Marc D 1519 LHOB 202-225-9897
34 Vela, Filemon D 437 CHOB 202-225-9901
35 Doggett, Lloyd D 2307 RHOB 202-225-4865
36 Babin, Brian R 316 CHOB 202-225-1555

Utah

District Name Party Room Phone
1 Bishop, Rob R 123 CHOB 202-225-0453
2 Stewart, Chris R 323 CHOB 202-225-9730
3 Chaffetz, Jason R 2236 RHOB 202-225-7751
4 Love, Mia R 217 CHOB 202-225-3011

Vermont

District Name Party Room Phone
At LargeWelch, Peter D 2303 RHOB 202-225-4115

Virgin Islands

District Name Party Room Phone
At Large Plaskett, Stacey D 331 CHOB 202-225-1790

Virginia

District Name Party Room Phone
1 Wittman, Robert J. R 2055 RHOB 202-225-4261
2 Taylor, Scott R 412 CHOB 202-225-4215
3 Scott, Robert C. D 1201 LHOB 202-225-8351
4 McEachin, A. Donald D 314 CHOB 202-225-6365
5 Garrett, Thomas R 415 CHOB 202-225-4711
6 Goodlatte, Bob R 2309 RHOB 202-225-5431
7 Brat, Dave R 1628 LHOB 202-225-2815
8 Beyer, Don D 1119 LHOB 202-225-4376
9 Griffith, Morgan R 2202 RHOB 202-225-3861
10 Comstock, Barbara R 229 CHOB 202-225-5136
11 Connolly, Gerald E. "Gerry" D 2238 RHOB 202-225-1492

Washington

District Name Party Room Phone
1 DelBene, Suzan D 2442 RHOB 202-225-6311
2 Larsen, Rick D 2113 RHOB 202-225-2605
3 Beutler, Jaime Herrera R 1107 LHOB 202-225-3536
4 Newhouse, Dan R 1318 LHOB 202-225-5816
5 McMorris Rodgers, Cathy R 1314 LHOB 202-225-2006
6 Kilmer, Derek D 1520 LHOB 202-225-5916
7 Jayapal, Pramila D 319 CHOB 202-225-3106
8 Reichert, David G. R 1127 LHOB 202-225-7761

9	Smith, Adam	D	2264 RHOB	202-225-8901
10	Heck, Denny	D	425 CHOB	202-225-9740

West Virginia

District	Name	Party	Room	Phone
1	McKinley, David	R	2239 RHOB	202-225-4172
2	Mooney, Alex	R	1232 LHOB	202-225-2711
3	Jenkins, Evan	R	1609 LHOB	202-225-3452

Wisconsin

District	Name	Party	Room	Phone
1	Ryan, Paul D.	R	1233 LHOB	202-225-3031
2	Pocan, Mark	D	1421 LHOB	202-225-2906
3	Kind, Ron	D	1502 LHOB	202-225-5506
4	Moore, Gwen	D	2252 RHOB	202-225-4572
5	Sensenbrenner, F. James	R	2449 RHOB	202-225-5101
6	Grothman, Glenn	R	1217 LHOB	202-225-2476
7	Duffy, Sean P.	R	2330 RHOB	202-225-3365
8	Gallagher, Mike	R	1007 LHOB	202-225-5665

Wyoming

District	Name	Party	Room	Phone
At Large	Cheney, Liz	R	416 CHOB	202-225-2311

List of State Governors

Governors are subject to change. District of Columbia residents should answer that D.C. is not a state and does not have a capital. Residents of U.S. territories should name the capital of the territory.

Source: http://en.wikipedia.org/wiki/List_of_current_United_States_governors January 2018

Alabama – Kay Ivey

Alaska - Bill Walker

Arizona - Doug Ducey

Arkansas - Asa Hutchinson

California - Jerry Brown

Colorado - John Hickenlooper

Connecticut - Dan Malloy

Delaware – John Carney

Florida - Rick Scott

Georgia - Nathan Deal

Hawaii - David Ige

Idaho - Butch Otter

Illinois - Bruce Rauner

Indiana - Eric Holcomb

Iowa – Kim Reynolds

Kansas - Sam Brownback

Kentucky - Matt Bevin

Louisiana - John Bel Edwards

Maine - Paul LePage

Maryland - Larry Hogan

Massachusetts - Charlie Baker

Michigan - Rick Snyder

Minnesota - Mark Dayton

Mississippi - Phil Byant

Missouri – Eric Greitens

Montana - Steve Bullock

Nebraska - Pete Ricketts

Nevada - Brian Sandoval

New Hampshire – Chris Sununu

New Jersey - Chris Christie

New Mexico - Susana Martinez

New York - Andrew Cuomo

North Carolina - Pat McCrory

North Dakota – Doug Burgum

Ohio - John Kasich

Oklahoma Mary Fallin

Oregon - Kate Brown

Pennsylvania - Tom Wolf

Rhode Island - Gina Raimondo

South Carolina – Henri McMaster

South Dakota - Dennis Daugaard

Tennessee - Bill Haslam

Texas - Greg Abbott

Utah - Gary Herbert

Vermont – Phil Scott

Virginia - Terry McAuliffe

Washington - Jay Inslee

West Virginia – Jim Justice

Wisconsin - Scott Walker

Wyoming - Matt Mead

List of State Capitals

Alabama - Montgomery

Alaska - Juneau

Arizona - Phoenix

Arkansas - Little Rock

California - Sacramento

Colorado - Denver

Connecticut - Hartford

Delaware - Dover

Florida - Tallahassee

Georgia - Atlanta

Hawaii - Honolulu

Idaho - Boise

Illinois - Springfield

Indiana - Indianapolis

Iowa - Des Moines

Kansas - Topeka

Kentucky - Frankfort

Louisiana - Baton Rouge

Maine - Augusta

Maryland - Annapolis

Massachusetts - Boston

Michigan - Lansing

Minnesota - St. Paul

Mississippi - Jackson

Missouri - Jefferson City

Montana - Helena

Nebraska - Lincoln

Nevada - Carson City

New Hampshire - Concord

New Jersey - Trenton

New Mexico - Santa Fe

New York - Albany

North Carolina - Raleigh

North Dakota - Bismarck

Ohio - Columbus

Oklahoma - Oklahoma City

Oregon - Salem

Pennsylvania - Harrisburg

Rhode Island - Providence

South Carolina - Columbia

South Dakota - Pierre

Tennessee - Nashville

Texas - Austin

Utah - Salt Lake City

Vermont - Montpelier

Virginia - Richmond

Washington - Olympia

West Virginia - Charleston

Wisconsin - Madison

Wyoming - Cheyenne

Avoid Scams

From the USCIS website: http://www.uscis.gov/avoidscams

The wrong help can hurt

Are you getting the right immigration help?

Many people offer help with immigration services. Unfortunately, not all are authorized to do so. While many of these unauthorized practitioners mean well, all too many of them are out to rip you off. This is against the law and may be considered an immigration services scam.

If you need help filing an application or petition with USCIS, be sure to seek assistance from the right place, and from people that are authorized to help. Going to the wrong place can:

Delay your application or petition

Cost you unnecessary fees

Possibly lead to removal proceedings

This site can help you avoid immigration services scams. Remember: Know the facts when it comes to immigration assistance, because the Wrong Help Can Hurt.

Tools to Help You Avoid Scammers

USCIS wants to combat immigration services scams by equipping applicants, legal service providers and community-based organizations with the knowledge and tools they need to detect and protect themselves from dishonest practices.

To accomplish this goal, USCIS launched the Unauthorized Practice of Immigration Law (UPIL) Initiative. As part of the effort, we've partnered with several government agencies to identify resources that can help you avoid immigration services scams.

Empower yourself by using our online educational resources, which include:

The top things to know before and after filing an application or petition

A list of common immigration services scams

State-by-state information on where you can report an immigration services scam

Advice on finding authorized legal help

Information on becoming an authorized legal immigration service provider

Educational tools you can print and share

This page can be found at: http://www.uscis.gov/avoidscams.

ABOUT THE AUTHOR

Mike Swedenberg saw a need to assemble a study guide to help those persons wishing to immigrate to the United States whose second language is English. This study guide is annotated with the names of current Representatives that all applicants must know. The list is current for State Governors, US Senators and US Congressmen. This list will be updated at each election cycle.

Other books by the Author
A New York Wedding – a novel
Bully Boss – a novel
The Road Warrior a sales manual
Advertising Copywriting and the Unique Selling Proposition
Smart Money Stupid Money – Advice
21 ½ Things to Know Before You Self Publish – Advice
How to Publish an eBook - Advice